Contain the Flame

Outdoor Fire Safety

How to Be Safe!

by Jill Urban Donahue   illustrated by Bob Masheris

PICTURE WINDOW BOOKS
Minneapolis, Minnesota

Special thanks to our advisers for their expertise:
Dave Pederson, Senior Ranger, Phillippo Scout Reservation
Northern Star Council, Cannon Falls, Minnesota

Terry Flaherty, Ph.D., Professor of English
Minnesota State University, Mankato

Editor: Jill Kalz
Designer: Abbey Fitzgerald
Page Production: Melissa Kes
Art Director: Nathan Gassman
Associate Managing Editor: Christianne Jones
The illustrations in this book were created digitally.

Picture Window Books
151 Good Counsel Drive
P.O. Box 669
Mankato, MN 56002-0669
877-845-8392
www.picturewindowbooks.com

Printed in the United States of America.

 All books published by Picture Window Books
are manufactured with paper containing at least
10 percent post-consumer waste.

Library of Congress Cataloging-in-Publication Data
Donahue, Jill Urban.
Contain the flame : outdoor fire safety / by Jill Urban
Donahue ; illustrated by Bob Masheris.
p. cm. – (How to be safe!)
Includes index.
ISBN-13: 978-1-4048-4820-7 (library binding)
1. Wildfires—Prevention and control—Juvenile literature.
2. Campfires—Safety measures—Juvenile literature.
I. Masheris, Robert, ill. II. Title.
SD421.23.D66 2008
628.9'22—dc22   2008006424

Campfires can be a lot of fun! They can toast your marshmallows and keep you warm. But they can also be dangerous. If you follow outdoor fire safety rules, you can make sure everyone has a great time.

3

Rico and his family choose a spot for their campfire. They pick a place that is out in the open. It is far away from trees, brush, and tents.

Rico's family wants to be safe.

Safety Tip

Before building a fire in a campground or park, check the rules. Different places have different rules about what kind of wood you can burn.

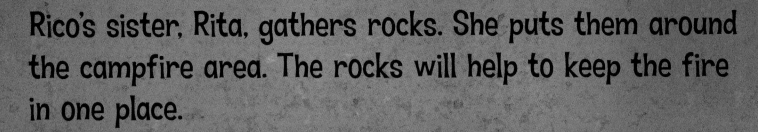

Rico's sister, Rita, gathers rocks. She puts them around the campfire area. The rocks will help to keep the fire in one place.

Safety Tip

Pick up any branches or leaves near the campfire area. That way, nothing will burn if a spark jumps out of the fire.

Rico walks to the lake. He fills a bucket with water. If the campfire gets too big, Rico and his family can use the water to put out the fire.

Safety Tip

Keep a bucket of sand and a shovel nearby. You can throw the sand on the fire to put it out. Use the shovel to dig up more sand or dirt as needed.

Mom gets ready to light the campfire. She crumples newspaper into balls. She stacks dry twigs and sticks around them.

Rico and Rita watch from outside the fire ring.

Safety Tip

Never light a campfire by yourself. Always have an adult with you.

Dad strikes a match and lights the newspaper.
He gently blows on it.

Safety Tip
Never play with matches.

As the campfire grows, Dad adds bigger sticks to it. He keeps the extra wood away from the fire.

Safety Tip

Don't let your fire get too big. The flames should be no higher than your waist.

Rita is hungry for toasted marshmallows. She and Dad go looking for long, straight sticks. Rico and Mom stay with the campfire.

Safety Tip

Make sure at least one person stays with your campfire at all times.

Other campers join Rico's family. Rico and Rita make sure their new friends don't get too close to the fire.

Safety Tip

If your clothes catch on fire, you must stop, drop, and roll. Stop moving, drop to the ground, cover your face with your hands, and roll to put out the flames.

A strong wind starts to blow. Windy weather can make campfires very dangerous. Sparks may fly far beyond the fire ring.

Rico helps Dad put out the campfire. They pour water over the logs. They throw scoops of dirt on top. Soon, the fire is out.

Rico and his family are careful with fire.
They are safe campers!

To Learn More

More Books to Read

Barraclough, Sue. *Fire Safety*. Chicago: Heinemann Library, 2008.

Cuyler, Margery. *Stop Drop and Roll*. New York: Simon & Schuster Books for Young Readers, 2001.

Raatma, Lucia. *Fire Safety*. Chanhassen, Minn.: Child's World, 2004.

On the Web

FactHound offers a safe, fun way to find Web sites related to topics in this book. All of the sites on FactHound have been researched by our staff.

1. Visit *www.facthound.com*
2. Type in this special code: 1404848207
3. Click on the FETCH IT button.

Your trusty FactHound will fetch the best sites for you!

Index

Look for all of the books in the How to Be Safe! series:

Contain the Flame: Outdoor Fire Safety

Play It Safe: Playground Safety

Ride Right: Bicycle Safety

Say No and Go: Stranger Safety